United States Government Accountability Office

Report to Congressional Committees

I0410963

July 2014

SECURITY FORCE ASSISTANCE

The Army and Marine Corps Have Ongoing Efforts to Identify and Track Advisors, but the Army Needs a Plan to Capture Advising Experience

GAO-14-482

GAO Highlights

Highlights of GAO-14-482, a report to congressional committees

SECURITY FORCE ASSISTANCE

The Army and Marine Corps Have Ongoing Efforts to Identify and Track Advisors, but the Army Needs a Plan to Capture Advising Experience

Why GAO Did This Study

SFA—DOD activities that contribute to supporting the development of foreign security forces and their supporting institutions—is a key component of U.S. efforts to create sustainable security around the world. These activities are carried out by DOD personnel serving as advisors who may have SFA-related training, education, and prior experience to conduct the advising mission.

GAO was mandated to review the Army's and Marine Corps' approaches to the SFA mission. GAO assessed the extent to which the Army and Marine Corps (1) identify and track personnel with SFA-related training, education, and experience and (2) consider SFA-related training, education, and experience in the promotion process. This report also describes the Army's process for preparing units to perform their core mission while some members are deployed to support SFA activities. GAO reviewed DOD policies, directives, and other documents and interviewed cognizant DOD and service officials.

What GAO Recommends

GAO recommends that the Army develop and implement a plan, with goals and milestones, for how it will develop the means for systematically identifying and tracking personnel with SFA-related experience. DOD partially concurred with the recommendation, stating that sufficient guidance and direction exists for the Army to continue refining its processes and procedures. GAO continues to believe the recommendation is valid, as discussed in the report.

View GAO-14-482. For more information, contact Cary Russell at (202) 512-5431 or russellc@gao.gov.

What GAO Found

The Army and Marine Corps have taken steps to identify and track personnel with Security Force Assistance (SFA)-related training, education, and experience, but the Army does not have a plan with goals and milestones to fully capture advising experience. A key element in conducting SFA missions is being able to identify the right personnel with the right training, education, and experience to execute SFA activities. The Department of Defense (DOD) established a requirement for the services to identify and track personnel with SFA-related training, education, and experience. Although the Army is able to identify and track soldiers with certain SFA-related training and education, it does not have a mechanism to identify and track SFA-related experience. Moreover, the Army has not developed a plan with goals and milestones on how it will capture this information. As a result, it is unclear how long it will take the Army to implement DOD's requirement and be able to readily identify the right personnel to serve in the SFA mission. The Marine Corps is implementing a mechanism to identify and track personnel with SFA-related training, education, and experience that is planned to be available in October 2014.

The Army and the Marine Corps have taken steps to ensure the consideration of SFA-related training, education, and experience in the promotion process. Both services have incorporated language into the guidance given to promotion boards to ensure that appropriate consideration is given to individuals who have served on advisor teams. However, opinions differ regarding the effect the guidance has had on the manner in which individuals with SFA-related training, education, and experience are considered during the promotion process. Some officials said that serving in an SFA role could potentially negatively affect career progression. Others noted that the promotion process considers the entirety of an individual's career and not just the time spent as an SFA advisor. However, because the Army and Marine Corps do not yet have comprehensive information on SFA advisors, officials are unable to determine whether promotion rates differ for people who served on SFA advisor teams versus those who did not. Such differences could be a potential indicator that servicemembers with SFA-related experience were negatively affected during the promotion process.

According to Army officials, the Army has taken a number of actions to ensure that units are prepared to perform their core mission when part of the unit is deployed in support of SFA activities. Officials stated that some actions taken to manage units that remain at the home station, also known as the rear detachment, when part of the unit deploys include consolidating units so that they can conduct training, ensuring the right personnel are left behind to lead the rear detachment, developing training plans for what the rear detachment would train to, and reporting on the availability of all personnel and equipment.

Contents

Abbreviations

DOD   Department of Defense
DODI   Department of Defense Instruction
MOS   Military Occupational Specialties
PDSI   Personnel Development Skill Identifier
SFA   Security Force Assistance

July 11, 2014

Congressional Committees

Security Force Assistance (SFA) is a key component of U.S. efforts to create sustainable security around the world. SFA is defined as Department of Defense (DOD) activities that contribute to unified action by the U.S. government to support the development of the capacity and capability of foreign security forces and their supporting institutions. Advising is a primary type of SFA.[1] Over the course of the military conflicts in Iraq and Afghanistan, as well as other locations, the Army and Marine Corps have used company- and field-grade officers and senior enlisted personnel[2] to form advisor teams to support SFA missions focused on advising and assisting partner-nation military forces.[3] Currently, to meet the requirements for SFA missions in Afghanistan, the Army deploys SFA brigades, which include advisor teams that are primarily created using personnel from the SFA brigade. The Marine Corps creates advisor teams using nondeployed personnel from across the Marine Expeditionary Forces[4] who then deploy as formed teams.

We have issued several reports about DOD's implementation of SFA. In 2013, we reported that the Army and Marine Corps have been able to fill

---

[1]Advising is the use of influence to teach, coach, and advise while working by, with, and through the foreign security force. Advising helps foreign security forces conduct independent decision making and operations, and advisors may also provide foreign security forces with direct access to joint and multinational capabilities, such as air support, artillery, medical evacuation, and intelligence.

[2]Company-grade officers are those in the pay grades of O-1 to O-3 (e.g., lieutenants and captains), and field-grade officers are those in pay grades O-4 to O-6 (e.g., majors, lieutenant colonels, and colonels). Senior noncommissioned officers are those in the pay grades of E-7 to E-9 (e.g., sergeants first class, first sergeants, and sergeants major).

[3]As we have previously reported, while the Army and Marine Corps have provided the majority of U.S. advisor personnel to Afghanistan, the Navy and Air Force also have contributed personnel to advise the Afghan National Security Forces. See GAO, *Security Force Assistance: More Detailed Planning and Improved Access to Information Needed to Guide Efforts of Advisor Teams in Afghanistan*, GAO-13-381 (Washington, D.C: Apr. 30, 2013).

[4]A Marine Expeditionary Force is a combined-arms force consisting of ground, air, and logistics forces that possesses the capability for projecting offensive combat power ashore while sustaining itself in combat without external assistance for a period of 60 days.

requests for SFA advisor teams using various approaches, such as tasking nondeployed brigades to form advisor teams or creating teams using personnel already deployed in Afghanistan.[5] We also reported that the Army's reliance on brigades to provide a portion of their personnel to form advisor teams has enabled them to meet requirements but has resulted in leaving large numbers of personnel at the brigades' home stations, known as rear detachments. To manage these large rear detachments, brigades have undertaken significant planning to ensure that enough stay-behind leadership existed to maintain a sufficient command structure and provide certain training. In 2012, we reported on the actions needed to guide geographic combatant commands and service efforts in regard to SFA.[6] Specifically, we reported that DOD had taken steps to establish its concept for conducting SFA, including broadly defining the term and identifying actions needed to plan for and prepare forces to execute it. We further reported that geographic combatant commands face challenges that limit their ability to plan for and track SFA as a distinct activity. In the 2012 report, we recommended that DOD develop or modify existing guidance that further defines the department's intent for SFA and what additional actions are required by the geographic combatant commands to plan for and conduct SFA beyond their existing security cooperation efforts. We also recommended that DOD take actions to ensure that updates to the Global Theater Security Cooperation Management Information System and the business rules being developed provide a mechanism and guidance to stakeholders to specifically identify and track SFA activities. DOD partially concurred with our recommendations, noting that it believed that the department had taken some steps to address some of the issues identified in our report. For example, DOD stated that additional guidance to the geographic combatant commands and services would be useful to promote understanding of SFA but noted that recently published strategic and planning guidance incorporated SFA planning requirements.

House Armed Services Committee Report 113-102[7] accompanying a bill for the National Defense Authorization Act for Fiscal Year 2014 mandated

---

[5]GAO-13-381.

[6]GAO, *Security Force Assistance: Additional Actions Needed to Guide Geographic Combatant Command and Service Efforts,* GAO-12-556 (Washington, D.C.: May 10, 2012).

[7]H.R. Rep. No. 113-102, at 127-128 (2013).

GAO to review the Army's and Marine Corps' approaches to the SFA mission. We assessed the extent to which (1) the Army and Marine Corps identify and track personnel with SFA-related training, education, and experience; and (2) the Army and Marine Corps consider SFA-related training, education, and experience in the promotion process. In addition, we describe the process the Army uses to prepare units to perform their core missions while some unit members are deployed to support SFA activities.

To determine the extent to which the Army and Marine Corps identify and track personnel with SFA-related training, education, and experience, we reviewed relevant policies, directives, and other documents and interviewed Office of the Secretary of Defense, Army, and Marine Corps officials to ascertain whether they have developed indicators to define SFA-related training, education, and experience and mechanisms for identifying and tracking personnel with such training, education, and experience. To determine the extent to which the Army and Marine Corps consider SFA-related training, education, and experience in the promotion process, we analyzed guidance and other documents that identify critical elements of a career path and reviewed guidance provided to promotion boards to instruct them on how to incorporate SFA-related training, education, and experience in their evaluation of individuals for promotion. In addition, we interviewed Department of the Army Headquarters officials from the Personnel and Operations and Plans directorates, Army Human Resources Command, Marine Corps Security Cooperation Group, and Marine Corps Manpower and Reserve Affairs. To describe the process that the Army uses to prepare units to perform their core missions when some unit members are deployed to support SFA-related activities, we reviewed documentation and interviewed knowledgeable officials from four selected SFA brigades to ascertain any potential readiness challenges to units having the ability to train and manage their readiness for core and assigned missions; and we reviewed what mitigation strategies, if any, they developed. We consulted with Army Forces Command officials to identify brigades that recently deployed as SFA Brigades. From the list these officials provided, we contacted brigades to identify which ones had a large rear detachment and had personnel available to speak with us. We then selected which brigades to visit. Officials from these brigades were also able to provide their perceptions of the effect that serving in an SFA-related role may have on promotion opportunities. We did not report on the readiness of the rear detachment for the Marine Corps because the Marine Corps' sourcing approach does not create the same type of large rear detachments that result from the

Army's use of SFA brigades. More detailed information on our scope and methodology is provided in appendix I.

We conducted this performance audit from August 2013 to July 2014 in accordance with generally accepted government auditing standards. Those standards require that we plan and perform the audit to obtain sufficient, appropriate evidence to provide a reasonable basis for our findings and conclusions based on our audit objectives. We believe that the evidence obtained provides a reasonable basis for our findings and conclusions based on our audit objectives.

Background

The Army and Marine Corps use established mechanisms that allow them to categorize and track personnel with specific skill sets. Specifically, each service uses Military Occupational Specialties (MOS) and additional skill identifiers to categorize the specific jobs and skill sets of officers and enlisted servicemembers. Department of the Army Pamphlet 600-3, Department of the Army Pamphlet 600-25, Department of the Army Pamphlet 611-21, and the Marine Corps' Military Occupational Specialties Manual outline the MOS and skill identifiers for officers and enlisted personnel.[8] The MOS describes a set of related duties and tasks that extend over one or more grades. For instance, infantrymen in the Army have an MOS of 11B, while those in the Marine Corps have an MOS of 03. Each MOS outlines a path for career development and management of each MOS by grade. This path helps direct the training, education, and experience that will guide a servicemember in career development, but it does not guarantee that individual's success. Instead, it describes the full spectrum of development opportunities that an officer or enlisted servicemember is expected to pursue throughout his or her career. For example, majors seeking promotion to lieutenant colonel in the field artillery branch of the Army are expected to continue their professional development by completing certain required military education and serving in key assignments such as fires brigade S3, as well as

---

[8]Headquarters Department of the Army, Department of the Army Pamphlet 600-3, *Commissioned Officer Professional Development and Career Management* (Washington, D.C.: Feb. 1, 2010); Headquarters Department of the Army, Department of the Army Pamphlet 600-25, *U.S. Army Noncommissioned Officer Professional Development Guide* (Washington, D.C.: July 20, 2008); Headquarters Department of the Army, Department of the Army Pamphlet 611-21, *Military Occupational Classification and Structure* (Washington, D.C.: July 2009); and Department of the Navy, Headquarters United States Marine Corps, *Military Occupational Specialties Manual,* MCO 1200.17E (Washington, D.C.: Aug. 8, 2013).

developmental assignments such as training developer. Further, these majors are expected to continue self-development efforts to build organizational leadership and strategic perspective, and to hone operational skills.

In addition to the MOS, a skill identifier is a career-management tool that identifies specific skills that are required to perform the duties of a particular position and are not related to any one branch, functional area, or career field. For example, all Army infantry officers who have met ranger training requirements will have a skill identifier of 5R, and those who have met parachutist training requirements will have a skill identifier of 5P. As servicemembers obtain additional skills not related to their primary skill set, they can be awarded an additional skill identifier associated with that skill set, based on their meeting criteria laid out in training standards or manuals. MOS and additional skill identifiers are maintained in the personnel data systems for the Army and Marine Corps and can be searched to identify personnel with certain experience.

The Army and Marine Corps Have Taken Steps to Identify and Track Personnel with SFA-Related Training, Education, and Experience, but the Army Does Not Have a Plan or Time Frame for Completion

DOD has established a requirement for the services to identify and track personnel who have completed SFA-related training, education, or experience in the Defense Readiness Reporting System with a relevant skill-designator indicating their SFA qualifications. According to Department of the Army headquarters officials, the Army has developed a mechanism to identify and track personnel who have completed certain SFA-related training and education and is considering steps to take toward identifying and tracking personnel with SFA-related experience, but it has not made a decision on what approach it will take. Further, the Army has not developed a plan with goals and milestones to identify and track personnel with SFA-related experience. The Marine Corps is in the process of implementing a means to identify and track individuals with SFA-related training, education, and experience.

DOD Has Established a Requirement for the Services to Identify and Track Personnel with SFA-Related Training, Education, and Experience

In October 2010, DOD issued an instruction—DOD Instruction (DODI) 5000.68— that broadly defines SFA and outlines responsibilities for key stakeholders to plan, prepare for, and execute SFA activities.[9] The instruction states that DOD shall develop and maintain the capability within DOD general purpose forces, special operations forces, and the civilian expeditionary workforce to conduct SFA activities in support of U.S. policy and in coordination with the relevant U.S. government departments or agencies. The instruction further states that DOD shall conduct SFA activities with the appropriate combination of general purpose forces, special operations forces, and civilian expeditionary workforce under a variety of conditions that include: (1) politically sensitive environments where an overt U.S. presence is unacceptable to the host-country government; (2) environments where a limited, overt U.S. presence is acceptable to the host-country government; and (3) environments where a large-scale U.S. presence is considered necessary and acceptable to the host-country government. The instruction further requires that the secretaries of the military departments identify and track individuals who have completed SFA-related training, education, or experience in the Defense Readiness Reporting System[10] with a relevant skill-designator indicating their SFA qualifications. According to DODI 5000.68, the secretaries shall develop, maintain, and institutionalize capabilities of servicemembers to support DOD efforts to organize, train, equip, and advise foreign military forces. Having the ability to identify and track individuals with SFA-related training, education, and experience will assist DOD in institutionalizing SFA capabilities. Officials at the Office of the Secretary of Defense, Department of the Army, and Headquarters Marine Corps stated that it was important to be able to identify and track servicemembers with SFA-related training, education, and experience so that they could be utilized for future SFA missions. Having this tracking capability will assist the Army and Marine Corps in identifying the right people to carry out SFA activities.

---

[9]Department of Defense Instruction 5000.68, *Security Force Assistance* (Washington, D.C.: Oct. 27, 2010).

[10]The Defense Readiness Reporting System measures and reports on the readiness of military forces and the supporting infrastructure to meet missions and goals assigned by the Secretary of Defense.

In April 2011, the Joint Requirements Oversight Council issued a memorandum[11] endorsing certain recommended SFA actions. As we reported in 2012, the memorandum identified 25 tasks related to the implementation of SFA across DOD in the areas of doctrine, organization, training, materiel, leadership and education, personnel, and facilities. According to SFA Working Group officials, this memorandum does not constitute policy. However, like DODI 5000.68, it emphasizes the need to identify and track personnel with SFA-related training, education, and experience. For example, one of the tasks that was emphasized for the services was the need to establish skill identifiers for military personnel with SFA-related training and experience, and the need to track these personnel. According to the memorandum, this task was to be completed by the Under Secretary of Defense for Personnel and Readiness, the services, the Defense Security Cooperation Agency, and United States Special Operations Command by April 2013. According to officials, an SFA Steering Committee and Working Group were established in January 2011 to coordinate the department's efforts to develop SFA policy and capabilities and manage the implementation of DODI 5000.68.[12]

According to officials with the Office of the Under Secretary of Defense for Personnel and Readiness, SFA continues to be a priority for DOD. As a result, officials stated that an instruction on irregular warfare[13] and SFA is being drafted in order to emphasize how DOD will conduct SFA activities. Among other things, according to officials, the instruction will reiterate the importance of identifying and tracking personnel with SFA-related training, education, and experience so that they can be utilized for future missions.

---

[11]The Joint Staff, *Security Force Assistance DOTMLPF Change Recommendation*, Joint Requirements Oversight Council Memorandum 050-11 (Washington, D.C: Apr. 19, 2011).

[12]These committees were dissolved in January 2014 and their functions are now encompassed in the Irregular Warfare Working Group.

[13]Irregular warfare is defined as a violent struggle among state and nonstate actors for legitimacy and influence over the relevant populations. It favors indirect and asymmetric approaches, though it may employ the full range of military and other capacities, in order to erode an adversary's power, influence, and will.

The Army Is Able to Identify and Track Personnel with Certain SFA-Related Training and Education, but It Lacks a Mechanism to Identify and Track SFA-Related Experience

The Army has taken steps toward identifying and tracking personnel with certain SFA-related training and education, but efforts to identify and track SFA-related experience are incomplete. Officials told us that since 2008, they have been identifying and tracking soldiers who attend certain SFA training with a Personnel Development Skill Identifier code. The Army uses Personnel Development Skill Identifier codes in combination with an area of concentration[14] or MOS to identify unique skills, training, and experience personnel may obtain during their careers.[15] Normally, the principal organizations or agency may request establishment of a Personnel Development Skill Identifier code for tracking unique skills, training, or experience where identification of qualified personnel would be beneficial to the Army. Personnel Development Skill Identifier codes identify skills, training, and experience that do not meet the minimum standards for establishment of an additional skill identifier or have too few individuals meeting the qualifications to warrant the creation of an additional skill identifier. For example, the Army has created Personnel Development Skill Identifier codes to identify and track soldiers who have completed congressional fellowship training, completed training and 6-month deployment in support of United Nations peacekeeping operations, and completed training for the maintenance of various weapons systems. With regard to certain SFA-related training and education, the Army has established Personnel Development Skill Identifier codes for the following training activities:

- successfully completing a resident advisor training course at Fort Riley and Fort Polk;

- successfully completing an advisor training course at the Phoenix Academy in Iraq; and

- successfully completing advisor training offered by the mobile training team from Fort Polk.

Army officials acknowledged that while these Personnel Development Skill Identifier codes can be used to identify and track soldiers who attend these SFA-related training courses, the codes do not identify and track

---

[14]Area of concentration identifies a requirement and an officer possessing a requisite area of expertise within a branch or functional area. An officer may possess and serve in more than one area of concentration.

[15]Department of the Army Pamphlet 611-21.

the actual experience that a soldier obtains from serving in an SFA-related role or any other SFA-related training and education that soldiers might receive. For example, according to an Army official, one brigade that is regionally aligned to Africa receives SFA-related training through a course called Dagger University at Fort Riley that is not captured by any of the existing Personnel Development Skill Identifier codes. Further, Army officials noted that some personnel trained in these activities might not have actually served in these roles.

Army officials stated that the Army has been considering steps to take toward identifying and tracking personnel with SFA experience, but has not yet developed a mechanism with which to do so. Officials from Department of the Army Headquarters Operations and Plans office stated that they have ongoing efforts to identify the best approach, which may include developing or expanding on existing Personnel Development Skill Identifier codes, or creating an additional skill identifier or MOS to meet the requirement in DODI 5000.68 to identify and track personnel with SFA-related experience. Army officials told us that they could create new SFA-related Personnel Development Skill Identifier codes or expand existing ones to identify and track personnel with SFA-related experience. The officials stated that they use a similar process to capture not only the education and training, but also the experience of individuals who have served in the Afghanistan-Pakistan Hands Program.[16] For example, Personnel Development Skill Identifier code T2A identifies soldiers who completed language, counterinsurgency, and culture training as part of that program. Personnel Development Skill Identifier code T2B identifies the soldiers who successfully completed a 1-year deployment to Afghanistan or Pakistan and utilized skills and training from the Afghanistan-Pakistan Hands Program. Officials indicated to us that they could potentially enhance existing SFA-related Personnel Developer Skill Identifier codes to capture the SFA-related experience of soldiers. However, as of the time of our review, Army headquarters officials stated that the Army had not decided which approach it would use. As a result, while they can identify personnel with certain SFA-related training and education, they have not developed a mechanism to identify and track personnel with SFA-related experience.

---

[16]The Afghanistan-Pakistan Hands Program was established in 2009 and deploys DOD civilians for 5 years to serve as experts on Afghanistan and Pakistan and to engage directly with host-nation officials to enhance government, interagency, and multinational cooperation in an effort to support the counterinsurgency strategy.

Army officials knowledgeable about these efforts told us that they have not yet determined what mechanism they might use to identify and track personnel with SFA-related experience for several reasons, including a lack of clarity regarding what activities and experience constitute SFA. For example:

- **Determining activities that constitute SFA.** According to officials from the Office of the Under Secretary of Defense Personnel and Readiness, SFA continues to evolve to meet emerging threats. Army officials stated that they are still trying to determine what activities constitute SFA. An Army headquarters official stated that identifying an activity as SFA is subjective and the Army is still trying to figure out how SFA fits into irregular warfare.

- **Determining SFA experience.** Army officials with whom we spoke stated that they are trying to determine the level of SFA responsibility that a soldier must assume in order for it to be recognized as sufficient for SFA experience and thereby tracked. For example, some individuals serve as junior members on SFA teams and may not continually engage in an advising role, whereas the leader of the SFA team is continuously advising foreign military officials.

Officials from the Under Secretary of Defense for Personnel and Readiness office told us they do not intend to issue any more prescriptive guidance to the services about SFA. Similarly, members of the SFA Working Group stated that the information available on SFA is adequate and they believe it is unnecessary to provide the services with any additional SFA guidance. We found several issued documents that define SFA or identify the characteristics that individuals conducting SFA activities should possess. These documents include the following:

- *The 2013 Army Field Manual on Army Support to Security Cooperation*, which provides details on the advisor roles, considerations for working effectively with foreign security forces, and personality traits of advisors. According to this manual, not every soldier is well suited to be an advisor.[17] It identifies tolerance for ambiguity, open-mindedness, and empathy, among others, as traits that greatly enhance the advisor's ability to adapt and thrive in a foreign culture.

---

[17] Headquarters Department of the Army, Field Manual No. 3-22, *Army Support to Security Cooperation* (Washington, D.C.: June 21, 2013).

GAO-14-482 Identifying and Tracking SFA Advisors

- *The Security Force Assistance Lexicon and Framework*, issued in November 2011, was intended to promote a common understanding of SFA and related terms by providing greater clarity on the definition of SFA and how it relates to other existing terms, such as security cooperation and security assistance.[18]

- *The International Security Assistance Force Guide 2.0*, which was updated in January 2014, defines SFA and provides information about advisor characteristics for the advising mission in Afghanistan.[19] According to this guide, not everyone is qualified to perform advisory functions. Similar to the Army Field Manual on Army Support to Security Cooperation, it identifies a tolerance for ambiguity, empathy, and open-mindedness, among others, as characteristics that will enhance an advisor's ability to adapt and thrive in a foreign culture.

- In January 2014, the Under Secretary of Defense for Personnel and Readiness issued a memorandum with guidance that identifies the common training standards for the SFA mission.[20] The memorandum lays out a list of skills—such as patience, adaptability, judgment, and initiative—related to SFA that are common across the forces, as well as standards that can be used as guidelines for measuring the qualifications of individuals and collective forces. It identifies a set of benchmarks for the services to use to identify, train, and track individuals and collective forces conducting SFA activities. For example, according to the memorandum, a servicemember should be proficient in cross-cultural communications, which include the ability to identify and discern cultural differences, and should demonstrate adaptability to engage in unfamiliar situations.

In 2012, we reported that combatant commanders lacked a clear understanding of SFA and therefore DOD made efforts to clarify the meaning of SFA.[21] In spite of DOD's efforts, Army officials with whom we

---

[18]Department of Defense, *Security Force Assistance Lexicon and Framework* (Nov. 1, 2011).

[19]International Security Assistance Force, Security Force Assistance, *ISAF Security Force Assistance Guide 2.0* (Kabul, Afghanistan: Jan. 1, 2014).

[20]Under Secretary of Defense for Personnel and Readiness, *Common Training Standards for Security Force Assistance Mission* (Washington, D.C.: Jan. 14, 2014).

[21]GAO-12-556.

spoke stated that confusion still remains regarding what constitutes SFA. According to SFA Working Group members, there may be a need for additional education regarding available resources that define and list activities that constitute SFA.

Although Army officials stated that the Army has considered steps to identify and track personnel with SFA-related experience, the Army has not established a plan with goals and milestones for how or when these steps will be completed. Since the Army does not have a mechanism to identify and track personnel with SFA-related experience, the Army would have to review duty descriptions in personnel files individually in order to determine which servicemembers have SFA-related experience. Manually reviewing files can be a laborious, time-consuming effort. Some DOD officials told us that it is not an efficient way to conduct business. Further, reviewing personnel files individually to identify servicemembers with SFA-related experience does not meet the requirement to identify and track individuals who have completed SFA-related training, education, or experience in the Defense Readiness Reporting System with a relevant skill-designator indicating their SFA qualifications. According to DODI 5000.68, individuals with SFA-related training, education, or experience were to be identified and tracked in the Defense Readiness Reporting System. However, since the Army has not established a method to identify and track personnel with SFA-related experience, this information is not being integrated into that system. Instead, personnel at Human Resources Command said they are able to manually review personnel files in order to identify servicemembers with SFA-related experience.

As noted above, the Army has not decided what approach it will take to identify and track personnel with SFA-related experience. Further, according to a headquarters Army official, no time frame has been set for meeting this requirement. Standard practices for project management call for agencies to conceptualize, define, and document specific goals and objectives in the planning process, along with appropriate steps, milestones, time frames, and resources to achieve those results.[22] Without goals and milestones, it is unclear how long the Army's implementation of the DODI 5000.68 requirement to identify and track personnel with SFA-related experience might take. As a result, the Army is at risk for not being able to readily identify the right personnel with the

---

[22]Project Management Institute, *A Guide to the Project Management Body of Knowledge* (PMBOK® Guide), 2000 ed. (Newtown Square, Pennsylvania: 2000).

right SFA-related skills and experience to serve in an SFA mission. This could potentially limit the effectiveness of the advisor teams and the Army's ability to develop, maintain, and institutionalize the capabilities of servicemembers to conduct SFA activities to build the capacity and capability of foreign military forces.

The Marine Corps Is Establishing a Free Military Occupational Specialty to Identify and Track Personnel with SFA-Related Training, Education, and Experience

The Marine Corps has approved and is in the process of implementing an officer and enlisted Free MOS to identify and track personnel with SFA-related training, education, and experience. A Free MOS is an auxiliary MOS that can be assigned to any Marine to reflect the acquisition of certain skill sets beyond those related to the primary MOS. Initially, in 2011, the Marine Corps developed an online irregular-warfare skills tracker to provide this capability, and the information in it was not readily accessible, could not be grouped by unit, and was not integrated with any other system in the Marine Corps. While the tracker met the intent of DODI 5000.68 to identify and track personnel with SFA-related experience and will be developed to meet emerging irregular warfare requirements, it was not sufficient in helping the Marine Corps assign servicemembers to SFA positions. As a result, in April 2013, the Marine Corps decided to develop a Free MOS that could be used to identify and track personnel with SFA-related training, education, and experience. The Marine Corps currently uses Free MOS to capture personnel with other skill sets and experience, such as personnel who have served as foreign area officers and regional area officers. The Marine Corps tasked its human resources command—Manpower and Reserve Affairs— as the lead to integrate the Free MOS into existing personnel systems in accordance with standard procedures for the creation of a new Free MOS.

In December 2013, the Commanding General of the United States Marine Corps Training and Education Command approved the Foreign Security Force Advisor Free MOS for officers and enlisted personnel. The Free MOS is currently being finalized and is expected to be included in the Marine Corps fiscal year 2015 MOS Manual.[23] The Marine Corps is planning for the Free MOS to be available by October 1, 2014, to assign to those Marines who meet specified qualifications. Those qualifications are identified as follows in the memorandum that approved the language for the Free MOS that will be added to the MOS manual:

---

[23]Headquarters United States Marine Corps, MCO 1200.17E.

GAO-14-482 Identifying and Tracking SFA Advisors

- **Prerequisites.** The Marine must complete the appropriate Regional, Culture, and Language training for that Marine's grade. In addition, the Marine must have an endorsement from a battalion- or squadron-level commanding officer certifying that the Marine has met the prerequisites, is mature, and is capable of independent operations.

- **Requirements.** The Marine must complete the Marine Corps Advisor Course. Alternatively, if the Marine does not complete the Marine Corps Advisor Course, the Marine can be certified by a commanding officer after demonstrating sufficient expertise in advising foreign security forces in an on-the-job training environment spanning a cumulative period of at least 6 months while still serving in the position.

According to the Marine Administrative Message that the Marine Corps has developed to announce approval of the Free MOS, Marines who have already graduated from an advisor course or who have 6 months or more of cumulative on-the-job experience advising foreign security forces may apply to be grandfathered in to receive the Free MOS. The Marine Corps Security Cooperation Group will convene a panel in order to review these applicants' packages, which should include a letter from the applicant to the commanding officer of the Marine Corps Security Cooperation Group, endorsement from battalion- or squadron-level or higher commanding officer, and documentation demonstrating that the Marine graduated from an advisor training course, among other things. The Marine Corps Security Cooperation Group is responsible for managing the Foreign Security Force Advisor MOS and the Marine Advisor Course. In the event that the Marine Corps Security Cooperation Group is disbanded, the Training and Education Command commanding officer would be responsible for determining who would provide the training going forward.

The Army and Marine Corps Have Taken Steps to Ensure the Consideration of SFA-Related Training, Education, and Experience in the Promotion Process

The Army and Marine Corps have established processes to guide and evaluate career progression. Both services have taken a number of actions to give consideration to those serving in SFA-related positions during the promotion process. However, DOD cannot evaluate the effect that serving in an SFA-related role could have on career progression because the Army and Marine Corps have not established a mechanism to identify and track servicemembers with SFA-related experience.

The Army and Marine Corps Have Established Processes to Guide and Evaluate Career Progression

The Army and Marine Corps convene promotion boards to review personnel for career advancement. These promotion boards consist of 5 to 21 servicemembers whose rank is above that of the promotion candidates. The promotion cycles for officers and enlisted personnel occur throughout the year. The promotion process is confidential, and each board member is briefed on and reviews the same information for each candidate, to include performance evaluations, assignment history, and professional development and education. According to DOD officials, board members review the entirety of servicemembers' careers when making decisions about promotions.

Both the Army and the Marine Corps provide guidance to promotion boards to assist them in their deliberations. Specifically, the Army provides every promotion board member with a Memorandum of Instruction signed by the Secretary of the Army for officers and the Army Chief of Staff for enlisted personnel. Similar to the Army, the Marine Corps provides every promotion board member with instructions, also referred to as precepts, that are signed by the Secretary of the Navy for officers and the Commandant of the Marine Corps for the enlisted personnel. According to the Memoranda of Instruction and precepts, promotion board members should not consider demographic information such as gender and ethnic background when making promotion decisions, as they have no bearing on servicemembers' merit and abilities. However, they should consider education, experience, and physical fitness in their deliberations. More specifically, for example, one of the Army's Memoranda of Instruction that we reviewed states that it is important that officers selected by board members for promotion possess the right mix of field and headquarters experience, as well as the training and education to meet current and future leadership requirements.

Further, it states that all assignments are important to sustain a trained and ready Army.

The Army and Marine Corps Have Taken a Number of Actions to Give Consideration to Those Serving in SFA-Related Positions during the Promotion Process

The Army and the Marine Corps have taken a number of steps to ensure that servicemembers with SFA-related experience receive consideration for serving in these positions during the promotion process. Both services have incorporated language into the guidance given to each promotion board member every time a promotion board is held to ensure that appropriate consideration is given to individuals who have served on advisor teams. For example, both the Army's Memoranda of Instruction and the Marine Corps' precepts for promotion boards state that, given the current operational environment, promotion board members should pay particular attention to servicemembers with unique key and developmental positions, to include serving on an advisor team.

Specifically, as it relates to SFA, one of the Army's Memoranda of Instruction states that the absence of command, combat experience, or support of deployed forces should not be a basis for nonselection for promotion. With regard to service as an advisor, the memorandum cites the important role that advisor teams play in enabling the United States to hand over security responsibilities to host-nation security forces and notes that advisor teams operate under very austere conditions and coach, teach, and mentor host-nation security forces while simultaneously conducting combat operations as they are embedded with host-nation security forces. The memorandum instructs the promotion board to appreciate the challenging nature of demands of advisor team jobs and to provide appropriate consideration in the overall evaluation of the record of each officer and enlisted servicemember who has served on these teams.

Similarly, the Marine Corps' precepts direct each promotion board to be especially diligent in weighing the qualifications of officers and enlisted personnel serving in advisor teams. They further state that, in board deliberations, service in these critical positions should be weighted equally with traditional Marine Corps officer and enlisted positions in the operational forces supporting overseas contingency operations because assignments are made in the best interest of the Marine Corps. To emphasize the importance of giving proper consideration to servicemembers who have served in SFA positions, according to a Marine Corps official, the Marine Corps is planning to draft additional language that will be briefed to members of each promotion board prior to their ranking of servicemembers for promotion.

In addition, according to an Army headquarters official, in an effort to ensure that servicemembers who serve on advisor teams are given credit for SFA-related experience, the Army made changes to its MOS publications. In 2008, the Army Chief of Staff stated that soldiers who served on advisor teams were developing the skills and experience that are vital for the Army to accomplish tasks from direct combat to stability operations, recognizing that these skills will be a major part of military operations in the future. To ensure that majors serving on advisor teams receive recognition and credit for their service, the Army Chief of Staff directed the Army to designate service on an advisor team as a key assignment for infantry majors in Department of the Army Pamphlet 600-3. For majors, serving on a brigade or battalion advisor team is therefore comparable to being assigned as, among other things, a battalion executive officer or brigade operations officer. According to an Army personnel official, the Army Chief of Staff's statement also served as a driver for the Army not only to change Department of the Army Pamphlet 600-3, but also to change Department of the Army Pamphlet 600-25, as well as the Memorandum of Instruction provided to promotion board members. The pamphlets have been updated to indicate that service in an advisor role is a key developmental opportunity. For example, the MOS of Army infantry majors and lieutenant colonels now reflect that service on advisor teams can be considered part of their key developmental assignments.[24]

Opinions Differ Regarding the Effect of Serving in an SFA-Related Position on Career Progression

We found differing opinions regarding the effect that Army and Marine Corps guidance have on the manner in which individuals with SFA-related training, education, and experience are considered during the promotion process. Several officials from the SFA brigades as well as officials at the Office of the Secretary of Defense, Army and Marine Corps headquarters, Human Resources Command, and Manpower and Reserve Affairs stated that serving as an SFA advisor could negatively affect career progression. Specifically, in 14 of the 24 interviews we conducted at these organizations, officials stated that serving in an SFA-related role could potentially negatively affect career progression, or that their own careers had been negatively affected as a result of serving in an SFA-related role. According to officials, serving in an SFA-related position could cause a

---

[24]A key developmental position is one that is deemed fundamental to the development of officer or enlisted personnel in his or her core branch or functional area competencies or deemed critical by the senior Army leadership to provide experience across the Army's strategic mission.

servicemember to miss or be delayed in completing a key developmental step outlined in the MOS publication, which could negatively affect the member's career progression. For example:

- One servicemember stated that he was taken out of company command to serve on an advisor team. This cut his company commander time down, which he believed made him less competitive compared to other servicemembers in his year group who had completed company command in accordance with the professional development outlined for his MOS.

- One soldier said that he wanted to apply for an opportunity that would allow him to transfer from a combat arms position into the Foreign Area Officer branch. According to the soldier, the time spent serving on an advisor team shortened the amount of time he could spend completing key developmental steps that were a prerequisite for him to transfer. The soldier stated that as a result of not completing the key developmental steps in his MOS, he did not qualify to apply for the transfer.

Conversely, some servicemembers with whom we spoke stated that they felt their careers had not been negatively affected. For example, one servicemember told us that he served on an advisor team and is now a colonel. He stated that serving in an SFA-related role is viewed in a positive manner and that soldiers seek these positions. Similarly, officials from the Army's Operations and Plans office stated that some soldiers' careers could potentially be enhanced as a result of serving in an SFA-related position.

In addition, officials from Army Human Resources Command and Marine Corps Manpower and Reserve Affairs, as well as officials from the Office of the Under Secretary of Defense for Personnel and Readiness, Department of the Army Headquarters, and the Marine Corps Security Cooperation Group, stated that other factors likely play into decisions not to promote an individual. They noted that the promotion process considers the entirety of an individual's career and not just the time spent as an advisor. According to the Army's MOS manual, success does not depend on the number or type of positions held, but rather on the quality of duty performance in every assignment. As a result, officials stated that serving as an advisor was unlikely to be the sole explanation for a failure to be promoted. According to officials, if a soldier performs well, that soldier will be promoted regardless of the role he or she was assigned.

According to DOD officials, it is difficult if not impossible to determine why a servicemember did not get promoted, because the promotion boards do not maintain a record of or discuss the reasons why a person did not get promoted. Officials from the Army Human Resources Command and the Marine Corps Manpower and Reserve Affairs Department informed us that they monitor where servicemembers are in their career to try to ensure that servicemembers are able to obtain a key developmental step that may be missed. Although some servicemembers stated that their careers could potentially be negatively affected as a result of serving in an SFA-related role, the Army and Marine Corps are currently unable to assess this potential negative effect or to take any needed corrective actions. Specifically, information about who has SFA-related experience is necessary in order to isolate this population from those who have not served in an SFA-related role. As noted above, while the Army has developed a Personnel Development Skill Identifier to identify and track soldiers with SFA-related training and education, the Army has not developed a mechanism with which to identify and track personnel with SFA-related experience, and the Marine Corps' mechanism will not be available until October 2014. As a result, officials are not able to conduct an assessment of personnel to determine whether there are different promotion rates for people who served on advisor teams versus those who did not, which could be a potential indicator that servicemembers with SFA-related experience were negatively affected during the promotion process.

The Army Continues to Manage the Large Rear Detachments That Result from Deploying Personnel to Support SFA Missions

We recently reported that the Army's use of SFA brigades to form advisor teams has enabled it to meet requirements, but this practice results in those brigades leaving behind large numbers of personnel at the brigades' home stations. Officials from each of the four SFA brigades with whom we met confirmed that this continues to be the case and said that they left behind a large rear detachment when they deployed. For example, according to officials from one of the brigades we visited, the brigade deployed approximately 500 people to create advisor teams, leaving approximately 3,000 personnel behind at their home station. Officials from another brigade that deployed as an SFA brigade stated that approximately 1,900 personnel were deployed, leaving behind about the same number in the rear detachment. In 2013, we reported that because the advisor team requirement calls for high numbers of company- and field-grade officers and senior noncommissioned officers, staffing the teams requires the brigades to deploy a significant portion of their leadership and expertise, including the brigade commanders and many battalion, company, and platoon commanders, for the advisor mission.[25] Army Forces Command officials confirmed that this continues to be the Army's process and that as a result, in providing these senior servicemembers to the advisor teams, the brigades are forced to rely on more junior officers and enlisted personnel at their home stations to manage the rear detachment. For example, according to SFA brigade officials we interviewed, in some cases they relied on captains, who would typically be responsible for leading a company, to serve as rear-detachment battalion commanders.

The rear-detachment commanders and other SFA brigade officials with whom we spoke stated they faced numerous challenges with managing personnel who were left at home stations. Officials from two of the SFA brigades we spoke with stated that their biggest challenge stemmed from effectively managing medical, legal, and other administrative issues while concurrently maintaining readiness and responding to installation tasks. These officials also stated that another challenge they faced was ensuring that equipment was accounted for properly.

During this review, officials from the SFA brigades we met with stated that the brigades' predeployment planning efforts ensured that the brigades left behind sufficient leadership to manage the rear detachments and develop training plans to maintain readiness. A number of other actions were also taken to maintain readiness that included the following:

- *Consolidating Units:* According to officials from two of the brigades we spoke with, to ensure that leadership is available to conduct training, some brigades consolidated units. For example, one rear-detachment battalion commander told us that his battalion teamed up with another battalion to ensure they could conduct training to maintain their readiness.

- *Leaving Key Leadership Personnel:* Officials told us that leaving the right personnel behind to manage the rear detachment is just as important as deploying the right personnel. Officials from the four SFA brigades we met with stated that brigade leadership had to undertake significant planning to ensure that the right leadership remained at the home station. One SFA brigade official with whom we spoke said that

---

[25]GAO-13-381.

rear-detachment leadership candidates were interviewed prior to being assigned as rear-detachment commanders to ensure that they had the personal and professional attributes needed to effectively manage the rear detachment. Officials from two of the SFA brigades we met with stated that the right leadership was needed to manage the training, legal, medical, and other administrative issues of the soldiers who remained at the home station.

- *Conducting Training and Maintaining Readiness:* Army Forces Command issued guidance for the training and employment of rear detachments during advisor team deployments, including missions the force may be assigned to, training expectations, and equipment maintenance responsibilities. According to Army Forces Command officials, Army Forces Command allowed the brigade leadership to determine the type and amount of training that could be conducted based on the number of personnel remaining at the home station. For example, officials from each of the four SFA brigades with whom we met stated that they developed training plans for what the rear detachment would train on while the rest of the brigade was deployed.

- *Reporting Readiness:* Prior to October 2013, brigades were required to report only on the status of deployed forces and equipment. The Department of the Army issued guidance in October 2013 to gain better visibility over all available personnel and equipment. It required units to report on personnel and equipment that were deployed and at the rear detachment. However, it is still up to the rear-detachment brigade leadership to determine the level of readiness that they can achieve with the personnel and equipment remaining at the home station.

Conclusions

SFA has been and continues to be an enduring part of the U.S. military effort in Afghanistan and other locations around the world. Accordingly, DOD wants to ensure that it has the ability to develop, maintain, and institutionalize the capabilities of servicemembers to provide SFA to foreign military forces. To ensure that the Army and Marine Corps have the right people with the right skill sets to serve in an SFA mission, DOD must be able to identify and track personnel with SFA-related training, education, and experience. Without a systematic means to identify and track personnel with SFA-related training, education, and experience, the Army and Marine Corps (1) cannot monitor the career progression of servicemembers with SFA-related experience; and (2) are limited in their ability to evaluate the effectiveness of their guidance. Currently DOD lacks this capability, and the Army has not developed a plan—including goals and milestones—to complete the implementation and institutionalization of its ability to identify and track personnel with SFA-related experience. Until the Army develops such a plan, it is at risk of not being able to readily identify the right personnel with the right skills and experience to serve in an SFA mission. Further, the absence of such a plan could limit the effectiveness of the advisor teams and DOD's ability to develop, maintain, and institutionalize the capabilities of servicemembers to provide SFA to foreign military forces.

Recommendation for Executive Action

To enable the Army to address the requirement to identify and track personnel with SFA-related experience, we recommend that the Secretary of Defense direct the Secretary of the Army to develop and implement a plan with goals and milestones for how it will develop the means for systematically identifying and tracking personnel with SFA-related experience.

Agency Comments and Our Evaluation

We provided a draft of this report to DOD for review and comment. In written comments on a draft of this report, DOD partially concurred with the report's recommendation. DOD's comments are summarized below and reprinted in appendix II.

DOD partially concurred with the recommendation that the Secretary of Defense direct the Secretary of the Army to develop and implement a plan with goals and milestones for how it will develop the means for systematically identifying and tracking personnel with SFA-related experience. In its letter, DOD stated that it concurred with our underlying assessment that the Army has had difficulty in systematically identifying and tracking personnel with SFA-related experience. However, DOD stated that sufficient guidance and direction exists for the Army to continue refining its processes and procedures. Specifically, DOD stated that the Army, through the application of its Personnel Development Skill Identifier (PDSI), is capable of identifying and designating all soldiers who have satisfactorily completed SFA training. DOD stated that it will continue to work with the Army in this important area.

We agree that the Army may have sufficient guidance to continue refining its processes and procedures. As noted in the report, the Army uses PDSI codes to capture certain SFA-related training activities; however, some SFA-related training and education may not be captured. Moreover, as noted in the report, the PDSI codes do not capture SFA-related experience. DODI 5000.68, which was issued in October 2010, requires the Army to, among other things, identify and track individuals with SFA-related training, education, and experience. As noted in the report, Army officials told us that they were discussing the best method to identify and track personnel with SFA-related experience, but the Army has not established a plan with goals and milestones to develop this capability. Such a plan will provide the necessary direction to enable the Army to develop the means for systematically identifying and tracking personnel with SFA-related training, education, and experience, as required by DODI 5000.68.

DOD also provided technical comments, which we incorporated as appropriate.

We are sending copies of this report to the appropriate congressional committees; the Secretary of Defense; the Secretary of the Army; and the Commandant of the Marine Corps. The report is also available at no charge on GAO's website at http://www.gao.gov.

If you or your staff have any questions about this report, please contact me at (202) 512-5431 or russellc@gao.gov. Contact points for our Offices of Congressional Relations and Public Affairs may be found on the last page of this report. Key contributors to this report are listed in appendix III.

Cary Russell
Director
Defense Capabilities and Management

List of Committees

The Honorable Carl Levin
Chairman
The Honorable James M. Inhofe
Ranking Member
Committee on Armed Services
United States Senate

The Honorable Richard J. Durbin
Chairman
The Honorable Thad Cochran
Ranking Member
Subcommittee on Defense
Committee on Appropriations
United States Senate

The Honorable Howard P. "Buck" McKeon
Chairman
The Honorable Adam Smith
Ranking Member
Committee on Armed Serves
House of Representatives

The Honorable Rodney Frelinghuysen
Chairman
The Honorable Peter J. Visclosky
Ranking Member
Subcommittee on Defense
Committee on Appropriations
House of Representatives

Appendix I: Objectives, Scope, and Methodology

The objectives of this engagement were to assess the extent to which (1) the Army and Marine Corps identify and track personnel with SFA-related training, education, and experience; and (2) the Army and Marine Corps consider SFA-related training, education, and experience in the promotion process; and to describe the process the Army uses to prepare units to perform their core missions while some unit members are deployed to support SFA activities.

To determine the extent to which the Army and Marine Corps identify and track personnel with SFA-related training, education, and experience, we reviewed relevant policies, directives, and other documents. The documents that we reviewed included the Department of Defense Instruction 5000.68, the *2013 Army Field Manual on Army Support to Security Cooperation, International Security Assistance Force SFA Guide 2.0*, and Marine Corps memorandum approving a Free MOS for SFA, as well as other memorandums as appropriate. We also interviewed officials from the Office of the Secretary of Defense, Department of the Army, and Headquarters Marine Corps, and personnel from Army Human Resources Command and Marine Corps Manpower and Reserve Affairs.

To determine the extent to which the Army and Marine Corps consider SFA-related training, education, and experience in the promotion process, we analyzed guidance and other documents that identify critical elements of a career path and reviewed guidance provided to promotion boards to instruct them on how to incorporate advisor experience in their evaluation of individuals for promotion. In addition, we interviewed Department of the Army, Headquarters Marine Corps, and service-level officials about the promotion process. We discussed their concerns about the potential negative effect of serving in SFA-related positions on their careers and the careers of others. Information that we received is not generalizable.

To describe how the Army prepares units to perform their core missions when some unit members are deployed to support SFA activities, we reviewed documentation and interviewed knowledgeable officials from four SFA brigades, and Army headquarters and service-level officials to ascertain any potential challenges to units having the ability to train and manage their readiness for core missions and mitigation strategies, if any, they developed. As part of this review, we selected an illustrative, nongeneralizable sample of brigades that sent SFA advisor teams to Afghanistan. We worked with Army Forces Command officials to identify brigades that recently deployed as SFA Brigades in Afghanistan and left a large rear detachment. Army Forces Command provided us with a list of five brigades that had recently served as SFA brigades in Afghanistan and had left a large rear detachment. From the list that it provided, we contacted the five brigades, but only four of them were available for us to interview. We could not conduct interviews with the fifth one due to conflicts with its deployment. From the four brigades that left a large rear detachment when they deployed and that were available to meet with us, we interviewed officials from the division, brigade, and battalion levels that were responsible for managing the rear detachment at each of the brigades we visited. We obtained testimonial evidence from the four selected brigades to ascertain any potential readiness challenges presented by the need to meet SFA requirements. Officials from these brigades were also able to provide information about their perceptions of the effect that serving in an SFA-related role has on promotion opportunities. We did not report on the readiness of the rear detachment for the Marine Corps because the Marine Corps' sourcing approach does not create the same type of large rear detachments that result from the Army's use of SFA brigades.

We visited or contacted officials from the following organizations during our review:

- Office of the Secretary of Defense, Arlington, Virginia
  - Personnel & Readiness
  - Military Personnel and Policy
  - Security Force Assistance Steering Committee and Working Group

- United States Army
  - Department of the Army Headquarters, Office of the Deputy Chief of Staff for Personnel (G-1), Arlington, Virginia
  - Department of the Army Headquarters, Operations and Plans (G-3/5/7), Arlington, Virginia
  - Human Resources Command, Fort Knox, Kentucky
  - 101st Airborne Division, Fort Campbell, Kentucky

    A. 1/101st Brigade Combat Team
    B. 2/101st Brigade Combat Team
    C. 3/101st Brigade Combat Team
    D. 1/101st Combat Aviation Brigade

- 3rd Infantry Division, Fort Stewart, Georgia
  - 1st Infantry Division, Regionally Aligned Forces, Fort Riley, Kansas

- United States Marine Corps
  - Marine Corps Security Cooperation Group, Arlington, Virginia
  - Manpower and Reserve Affairs Department, Quantico, Virginia

We conducted this performance audit from August 2013 to July 2014 in accordance with generally accepted government auditing standards. Those standards require that we plan and perform the audit to obtain sufficient, appropriate evidence to provide a reasonable basis for our findings and conclusions based on our audit objectives. We believe that the evidence obtained provides a reasonable basis for our findings and conclusions based on our audit objectives.

Appendix II: Comments from Department of Defense

OFFICE OF THE ASSISTANT SECRETARY OF DEFENSE
4000 DEFENSE PENTAGON
WASHINGTON, D.C. 20301-4000

READINESS AND FORCE
MANAGEMENT

JUN 24 2014

Mr. Cary Russell
Director, Defense Capabilities and Management
U.S. Government Accountability Office
441 G Street, NW
Washington DC 20548

Dear Mr. Russell:

This is the Department of Defense (DoD) response to the GAO Draft Report GAO-14-482, "Security Force Assistance: The Army and Marine Corps Have Ongoing Efforts to Identify and Track Advisors but the Army Needs a Plan to Capture Advising Experience," dated May 20, 2014 (GAO Code 351846).

The Department is providing official written comments (attached) for inclusion in the report.

Sincerely,

Laura J. Junor
Deputy Assistant Secretary of Defense
Readiness

Attachment:
As stated

GAO DRAFT REPORT DATED MAY 20, 2014
GAO-14-482 (GAO CODE 351846)
"Security Force Assistance: The Army and Marine Corps Have Ongoing Efforts to Identify and Track Advisors but the Army Needs a Plan to Capture Advising Experience"

DEPARTMENT OF DEFENSE COMMENTS
TO THE GAO RECOMMENDATION

RECOMMENDATION 1: The GAO recommends that the Secretary of Defense direct the Secretary of the Army to develop and implement a plan with objectives and milestones, for how it will develop the means for systematically identifying and tracking personnel with SFA-related experience.

DoD RESPONSE: Concur in part with this recommendation. We concur with the underlying assessment that the Army has had difficulty in systematically identifying and tracking personnel with SFA-related experience, however sufficient guidance and direction exists for the Army to continue refining their processes and procedures. The Army, through the application of their Personnel Skill Development Identifier (PSDI), is capable of identifying and designating all soldiers who have satisfactorily completed SFA training. We will continue to work with the Army in this important area.

Appendix III: GAO Contact and Staff Acknowledgments

GAO Contact	Cary B. Russell, (202) 512-5431 or russellc@gao.gov
Staff Acknowledgments	In addition to the contact named above, James A. Reynolds, Assistant Director; Emily Biskup; Richard Burkard; Michael Silver; Sonja Ware; and Cheryl Weissman made key contributions to this report.

Related GAO Reports

Security Force Assistance: More Detailed Planning and Improved Access to Information Needed to Guide Efforts of Advisor Teams in Afghanistan. GAO-13-381. Washington, D.C.: April 30, 2013.

Building Partner Capacity: Key Practices to Effectively Manage Department of Defense Efforts to Promote Security Cooperation. GAO-13-335T. Washington, D.C.: February 14, 2013.

Afghanistan: Key Oversight Issues. GAO-13-218SP. Washington, D.C.: February 11, 2013.

Afghanistan Security: Long-standing Challenges May Affect Progress and Sustainment of Afghan National Security Forces. GAO-12-951T. Washington, D.C.: July 24, 2012.

Security Force Assistance: Additional Actions Needed to Guide Geographic Combatant Command and Service Efforts. GAO-12-556. Washington, D.C.: May 10, 2012.

Iraq and Afghanistan: Actions Needed to Enhance the Ability of Army Brigades to Support the Advising Mission. GAO-11-760. Washington, D.C.: August 2, 2011.

Please Print on Recycled Paper.

www.ingramcontent.com/pod-product-compliance
Lightning Source LLC
Chambersburg PA
CBHW080734290526
45790CB00008B/3191